Outstripping Gravity

Other books by the author:
Learning Not to Touch (Redbeck Press, 1998)
Reaching for a Stranger (Shoestring Press, 1999)

Outstripping Gravity

Michael Tolkien

RED BECK PRESS

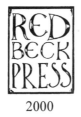

2000

Outstripping Gravity is published by:
Redbeck Press, 24 Aireville Road, Frizinghall
Bradford, BD9 4HH

Design by Tony Ward
Printed at the Arc & Throstle Press,
Nanholme Mill, Todmorden, Lancs.

ISBN 0 946980 75 6

ACKNOWLEDGEMENTS
Earlier versions of some of these poems have appeared
in: *Agenda, Envoi, Iota, Leicester Poetry Society Antholo-
gies 1998 & 1999, Orbis, Other Poetry, Poetry Notting-
ham, Poetry Now, Prop, Seam, Staple, Tabla 1998, Tears
in the Fence, The Affectionate Punch, The Interpreter's
House, The Penniless Press, The Rialto, The Swansea Re-
view, This is.*

Thanks are due to Shoestring Press for permission to
include two poems from *Reaching for a Stranger,* and
to Tom Tolkien for assembling some of these poems in
publishable form (as *Turn of the Tide*) for the East
Midlands Arts New Voices Tour (1998)

The author is especially grateful to John Forth and Paul
McLoughlin for their detailed and challenging appraisals
and suggestions.

The cover illustration is from a painting by Dorothy
Hardy in *The Book of Myths* by Amy Cruse (Harrap:
1925). Thiassi carries off Loki attached to the stick with
which he attacked the disguised Storm Giant.

Redbeck Press acknowledges financial assistance
from Yorkshire Arts Board

CONTENTS

For Jan,
Cathy, Tom and Ruth

'Two errors: first, to take everything literally;
secondly, to take everything spiritually…'
(Blaise Pascal: *Penseés*: 1670)

1

LANDSCAPE WITH TREES

MAKING A LIVING

I.

Glimpsed from a car, that winter flock
of rooks and crows are burnt paper
strips flapping on the wind's
back from a fire of sacks and sticks.

The lookouts perch in hedgerow ashes,
still as buds or growths. Others
prod round wheat needles striped
by trailing wings of pesticide.

We steer without seeing, speed
away from invented disturbances,
catch a whiff of the land
they've no choice but to peck at.

II

When he was inspecting his cattle,
doing sums while they stuffed their heads
in hay, I wanted him to care
whether they fed and breathed easily,
lacked water after a long drought.
But I could only say: 'Some are down
beyond, missing the party.' And he grinned:
'They'll come quick enough when I call.'

Next day a path of flattened docks and thistles
led from double gates to a truck on the verge.
It rocked as twenty bullocks jostled for standing room,
pressing their hides through its slats.
The driver sat in the sun eating a pie
while his engine cooled with reassuring ticks.

HOLDING OUT

When Rutland turned arable, he'd kept to
wintering *yows*, took on lean, high-strung
Euro-breeds, though even with native
beasts you could take nothing for granted.

One of his Herefords got clean over pens,
dented a locomotive, buckled a stockman's
steel leg, and cleared Harboro's streets
like a curfew till they slashed its hams:
a contest he chuckled over, looking straight
at you with words weathered as his clothes,
shaping and slicing a yarn like his hedges,
laid to be feet thick within three years.

He made an art of twine jobs, hand-grubbed
every dyke, clearing the smoke of thorns
from his eyes to greet you with time enough
for putting neighbours and pasture to rights.

INSIDE OUT

This self-styled tramp prefers old clothes,
boots that keep out the wet to casuals
made to look good in a precinct.
When afternoon TV turns from *Weather*
to *Westerns,* even if it's blowing rain or snow
hard over surfaces and hair, he'll be out.

Once he said he'd have come in sooner, but found
untrodden snow to make fresh prints as far
as the fence he calls the verge of *Nowhere*,
just before fields and hedges drop in folds
with nothing to hide. Then retracing his tracks
he'd matched them stride for stride.

NO ESCAPE

After I've sweated across ditches and rutted pasture
forestry closes in, my corduroys playing tunes
along its alleys. I hold my breath,
convinced there's an answering whistle
from bushes that crawl among spruces
contractors leave untrimmed –

coverts foxes slip from to pick off pheasants
just released and wondering where to scratch.

I find spent cartridges, their precision-kill
codes mellowing to ochre, flesh-rose, sepia, jade.

RETREAT

This is where fields bit back at the wood
baring the post and arms of an old pen

till fertiliser bags were dumped
and weeds flared up taller by the year,

choking a corner where threshers left
heaps of straw to steam and rot till Spring.

Then rogue barley, pink bindweed and heartsease
scabbed the wound of its burning.

Now I've been told a forester who coppiced
these overhanging ashes felled himself

I keep clear, wondering whether to lift
lichened remnants to a cross.

AFTER THE DOWNPOUR

Watching clouds blown to rags across
a widening blue and dazed by spaces
light opens up, we've lost the horse
and pony. Making your hands binoculars
you spot them set on fire by low sun,
drooping near a rusted manger, haunches
turned to a gale that plastered their hides,
steaming now in air that's close to freezing.

When we call they blame each other,
smacking their heads together. The black
trap-pony's content to meet your breath,
but the horse shakes its damaged back
and makes as if to graze: a thickset
muddy bay all of twenty five, his face
the longer for its white crack, he asks
for more than we had brought.

HEREDITY

Beyond their *Ha-Ha*, Park Wood hides the old mines.
Peacocks strut among gardeners. Swallows
loyal after more than seven hundred summers
dip over fishponds they've just restocked.

They used to dress like peacocks and winter
abroad like swallows. Nowadays they're all
creases and pleats to fit the City, the House
on telly, their new-fangled Roller.

Anyway, they've fixed up waterfalls, adventure
copses, herbs and seasonal colours, hired
reliable waterfowl, secured their perimeter.
Time to open up, find out what they're worth.

CEFFYL DŴR

...vipereos dentes, populi incrementa futuri. (Ov. Met.iii:103.)

This gorge cuts into cultivated patchwork.
Some say mold from under its rotting alders
fermented Ceffyl Dŵr. Part horse, part reptile,
it slunk into swamps far below
and reared up like a cresting wave
to flatten anything that moved.

Strange that from teeth it left behind
there sprung a tribe that had no taste for
war or treachery, and never left the hills.
They founded forest cults, let swine root
through oak scrub and hunted predators
from zig-zag paths their cattle made.

The valley was sedge in summer, marsh in winter.
Now opening time's the arbiter.
On scattered farms meals are left to stew,
while men drink to quarterly deals
that cook the books, crushing complaints
under monstrous wheels that churn them home.

Note: *Ceffyl Dŵr (Water Horse)*: local Clwyd variant of the Red Dragon *(Ddraig Gôch).*

15

HOISTING AND GROWTH

1

A gantry crane's constructing holiday
apartments. Its empty angles cap three
eucalypti spurting eighty foot from rock
and rubble. They seem to cradle a block
balancing the slender bridge that trundles
a dripping tank over the heads of roofers
who cheer and open their arms.

Hearing a weary, froglike *ribbit-ribbit*
you know it's straining into finer adjustments.
But swivelling full circle it's a one-winged goose
that honks for bearings among mist-covered ravines.

2

If they calculate at all eucalypti expect
no results. 'Well-covered' in more senses
than the Greek, protean in leafing and mating,
they're one-scene props you can't wheel off.
To sketch these giant myrtles you need a free
wrist and soft pencils and where do you stop?

As for capturing a crane's proportions,
try it without a 6H and steel rule.
Every particle, rivet, ratio between cog
and twine is reliably computed to several
decimal points. But the operator's no
button-pusher. Knowing how a slight breeze
or shift in temperature upsets his charge,
he tweaks its harness in trial and error.

LEAVETAKING*

A wheeling smudge high up is lapwings
tucked tight against a hawk,
shredding at the all-clear to touch
down at once, though each takes
its own time to settle wings
three times the length of a body
made to dart on wader's legs.

Eyeing them in by tens, I score
a hundred crests, but out of nowhere
other flocks unfurl and deflate
their striped banners until
in awe at being complete,
all go still. Even starlings
hobnobbing there forget to quarrel.

Then they unwind into grubbing,
make a show of preening,
or mew at those that chuckle
three feet up like half-fledged chicks.
But a tremor from the margins
tenses them to watchfulness so

intent they melt without
movement round six bowlegged rams
grazing through their conference:
fields away from estates and roads
yet open for miles to the west
beyond the reach of a bird's eye.

* '...in autumn lapwings congregate, often in flocks of many hundreds, and even
thousands; and no doubt...a large proportion of birds that breed with us leave the
country...' (W.H. Hudson: BRITISH BIRDS)

17

TRANSFIXED

Baring sodden earth from under five years' growth
I'm inspected by a blackbird, mother to a second
brood. She pokes my clods of writhing tubers,
tames me into slow motion and loses patience.
Foraging through leaves she sets off squeals:
a gored frog minus a leg leaps out, flailing
round and shrill with agony till the final
skewering dispatches it to ready morsels.

I feel dismembered and meddling might put me
next in line, fitter prey than this jelly
digested jab by jab to inject five yellow shrieks,
not to mention mashed worm and woodlouse
left in a parcel by my abandoned spade.

WITHOUT TOOTH AND CLAW

Going out for milk I notice slicks
of cat crap on grass and rockery
where small-hour yowling woke us
to murder. Finding no fur I blamed
piebald Thermal, so christened for his purr.
Neutered but not shorn of bully genes
he spat and growled at rivals half his size
till they shat their fear from lawn to rock and fled.

He'd pick on Stroker, little black
with a starry-cheeked smile. I've seen her
harried by blackbirds across two walls and over
a six-foot gate to land in splay-foot panic.

As for her po-faced stalker, my dream raptor
strikes just when he's unloaded where I've raked,
slinking off without a gesture of burial.

APRIL MALLARDS

'There's no more valour in that Poins than in a wild duck...' (H.IV 1,2,ii.)

Drake and duck splash up from hidden dew ponds,
fly north and wheeling back high overhead,
spot me taking root among leafless saplings.

After a field's width they veer east out of sight,
return west towards the floods below, bank
at the sudden void, swooping low to assess

what menaces the fresh pool, swerve, sway apart,
then go south side-by-side across a hedged
horizon. All without one note of panic.

Minutes later my head's still in a watery sky
when the drake quacks north on whistling wings.
Have they fallen out? Is it rage and grief

at seeing her striped smile crumple against
a rogue cable before she plummeted from air's
assurance, leaving him to test a polar wind?

LANDSCAPE WITH TREES

Even walking this sandy heath
    can't wash us clean
of the same old poets. Brushing past
    gorse, you snipe at
names made for topicality,
    Colossi no one assails.

Then our path's a timber causeway
    over marsh restocked
with reed and sedge, a sanctuary
    no birds frequent.
True to their suspicions or
    untouched by fashion

they've taken to firs and brambles
    round a hotch-potch house
so derelict we stop to steal
    the peace of its jungle
till late-sleeping tenants open
    their shutters on our dreams.

But when we wind round oaks
    in rotting ferns,
you insist they're stalwarts who stand
    their ground, and stop to
hug your favourite. I toe
    holes in leaves and hold

a branch for company, watching
    the embrace of mortals
who seize the moment and cling
    to life at all costs.
Flesh and centuries-hard rind
    with nothing to exchange.

HELENEN VALE

We walk the forest downstream
to Baden. Shelves of rock weathered
white, loom through trees, their scars
hollowing to caves as they tower nearer
and squeeze us onto a ledge above the river.

Calmly you explain these slabs and why
they block our way, as if to your girls,
who'd listen and remember, as I do,
hearing finches and a nuthatch freshly
metallic for spring, our boots kicking up
winter leaves strewn across the path
called '*Beethoven's Walk*'.

Devoured with knowing what it was to hear,
he saw Prometheus in chains up there.

CLOSE TO THE WIND

We were two names in a guided walk
the day Spring strafed the Wienerwald,
snapped limbs of beech like sticks,
swirled dust and leaves down rutted tracks
and over banks of primrose and violet,
blew out the palpitating sun and lit
outriding trunks in a blaze of sleet.

Nimbler than the others, we too went
on the rampage, but so intent on feet
and heads, dismissed our eyes' split-
second *Yes*, threw confidence to the gale,
and let it hurl us in a downhill race
till the clatter of quicker and shorter
steps assumed a pace we couldn't resist.

IMPERIAL CHILL

Snow falls steadily on coach parties
queuing in Maria Theresa's stable yard
to tour her summer suite. She'd note
our footprints absconding past avenued canals
and up the slow *S* to the Gloriette, whose eagle
triumphs over porticos of scaffold and screens,
and peers at palace wings hazing into
sepia parks.
  Our hearts freeze
until we cross a kind of border into woods
where squirrels caper round for snacks,
and small birds brush our shoulders to remind
us of their due. Snow seeping through in tatters,
clings to curls your hood's released,
melting gently down your tightened brow.

OASIS

A buzzard wails over its tidy acres.
Miles of gravel thread ranked conifers
and fields shorn by ewes that rattle
their caked-on faeces at me. Suddenly
I sink into ruts below tall ashes.
Shade simmers with ventriloquies
of water under moss and fern, flies
seesaw high among shafts of light.

The map says **Fron Gelyn**, *Hillside of the Enemy.*
Contours thicken with harder miles ahead,
rising to **Moel Famai**, *Mother of Hills.*

Histories I fold away to press on
with my own, like any fugitive.

PONT Y MWYNWR

Where the miners' bridge crosses the sluggish Alun
I've hired a cottage with bowed slate roof, walls feet
thick, mismatching windows. It stays cool even in July,
so I'm given coal, and told that fires are company.

But it's glad to have you here, listens to whatever
comes to mind, hides nothing round corners. Move
trinkets and furniture, be as nosey as you like,
open every drawer. Spread yourself. Whistle.

Outside it's a cracked face stained with gutter
rust and stalactites of swallow shit, but set
on a shoulder of tussocks and alders that root
in its heart, fending off the worst of the north.

Across a tarmac yard starred with camomile,
an outhouse called *The Groom's* shows the way
it might go, loosening stone green as beech trunks,
elder rocketting through its last few rafters:

hard to imagine as sparrows settle into their eaves,
black fly and moths smack the glass, forcing the door
as if my light's a matter of life or death. One squirt
would shoot the lot, yet here they are visitors

from woods so steep there's no dawn, only jackdaws
nattering in spirals, croaking splashes of coots
rippled across my ceiling. But still no swallows,
none since the owners went their separate ways.

MARKING TIME

BLUEPRINT

From this open place the land drops
to a tree-lined dyke, rises into the arms
of Gallows Wood, and levels to acres of crops.

Beyond, the west inks out a belt of hills,
Burn, Knob and Dick, exclusive to rotation
or cattle, map names, nowhere to mention.

Northward lie blunter ridges too surly
for names to stick, hammerheads of a valley
that's lengthened its shadows over the years.

*

ROSEHIPS

Saw-tooth groins of Dogrose end
a hedge by hilltop gates where fields meet
    and fall a hundred feet.

It flowers for a day or two in June
but never fails to juice its finger tips
    with a shower of hips.

November cuts into your wrapped stem
as you pick them for another daughter
    fourteen years later.

Snagging your palms is a pact with eyes
that shine for berries, but up here you're far
    from knowing which pair.

2

PROXIMITIES

HEADS

The sea is gloom, smothers
its breaking below shingle banks.
I slither down and find a strip
of sand, stones washed to a glitter.

The sea opens its claws and barks.
It's your beast. You tame it.
I miss your seal head shining,
dipping, feet splayed to a fish tail.

One stone longs for you. Dog's head
in bleached blue with a probing eye.
Its lustre dries in my hand,
and I hear your disappointment.

You'll never be too old for stones,
though you're putting a date on me.

RESPONSIBLE

A small square envelope leans on the sugar bowl:
'*To Mum & Dad*' in cramped blue biro.

Inside three mice suspended from a stalk
make a rope of torsos and tails for the third
to reach a berry.

It couldn't be us, could it, taking the strain
to let the one we love make a safer picking?

What's said inside should cut me down for
making light of that, if it didn't make me
hold on harder.

*Thanks for putting up with me. Sorry if I've made
life miserable. Your annoying daughter,*
   X Jackie X

27

RETINITIS

In a dimmed consulting room she's high
above us in a swivel chair, surrounded
by gadgets. Eyes wide from drops she dreads
strain after a shadow craning over her
with disc after disc. Holding them close he fires
his torch from every angle as if to gauge
the chinks or probe for clearance and caving in.

His smile meant for us or her must signal
new light. But it's 'no change'. Her lease
is renewed, and details of what's next or who
to consult cluster like tendrils across our view.

In the gardens she races after pigeons to share
her crisps. Grabbing one fantail for a closer look
she scatters the lot and releases us with laughter.

HERBS FOR THE KITCHEN

You gave me lavender
and weeds stuffed headfirst
into a brown paper bag,
tugging its neck tight
with a child's *forever.*

'To peg up in your kitchen
and make it smell nice.'
Ten years drying on a nail,
and as I take it down
ready for the decorator

the shrivelled mass bursts
its grease-worn belly:
dust of you at seven
wearing each day's bracelet
of unexpected charms.

Now though you're snared
by exams, the future, Sex.
You've gone from dressing
dolls to fretting over
weekends and hair

each idol changes,
leaving me with a knot
of paper shreds to wait for
your peep around the door,
the *hello* that means *goodbye.*

KATIE'S NEW HOUSE

boldly heads your letter typed
on the green of unpolluted shallows.
All the rage for fifties bathrooms,
and Mum's choice for whitewood cabinets.
I wonder what colours you'll wake to

and live with till you drape weekends
in dustcovers and overalls, spreading
fumes the pros say retire them early
but make us feel fresh and clean,
like aerosolling after fry-ups.

I've found you in a maze of oblongs.
Ivy Road, 52, makes me feel my age
and see your hands on a brass knob pushing
against a door that glints racing green
under veils of variegated creeper.

FAIR DEAL

"Very fair deal," says a bird on the ridge tile.

Daddy's bought daughter the end terrace house.

Outside she parks her brand new buggy,
purest white.

"Springtime's pretty," says a bird in the gutter.

Driving anywhere any minute
makes her little bottom sag.

"Pretty fair," say the birds.

Lads would have to pay for what she did behind
Dad's conifers. Now there's plenty going free.

"Springtime's your pretty ringtime",
laughs a bird on the patio.

But anyone who thinks he's well astride
soon finds she's had her fill.

"Fair deal..."

And Daddy hasn't a clue. He's very big in mixed fibres.

"Pretty spring patterns."

As for Mummy, no bird remembers, and daughter's
driving on past spring.

"It's a deal!" Scream the birds.

SENTENCED

At playtime he moons about kicking stones
or sucks up to younger lads, punching
chirpy ones who make him feel a fool.

'Don't pick on me, you fucking wanker,'
he warns teachers who've run out of ways
to make him tidy up and settle down.

His dad's doing eighteen months
for interfering with him. The silence could be
worse, staff avoiding it with looks,

kids drilled not to bring it up,
his mum too feeble not to take it
out on him by spoiling the youngest,

a sister he defends like a mastiff.
It was all they could do to stop him choking
a girl who started slagging her off.

PARENTAL BACK-UP

Dick's adopted. Dream prodigy who rips
through Maths like *let's pretend*, and writes
neat four-letter words on cardigans and cuffs.

Dick's in trouble. His mum's parked at the gates.
Not often you see a school governor all dolled up
and waiting to welcome kids off the bus.

Dick does a bunk. Later, cleaners find assorted
playing cards backed with a female nude. Small fry
for the Head who bins them with a yawn.

Dick's almost off the hook. But his mum says
the pack belonged to friends, only to be told,
in case she didn't know, that there are rules.

Dick had dealt out Spades and most of Diamonds
on the bus. 'Serves her right.' one teacher said.
'Who did the woman on the cards remind you of?'

32

FIDDLING

They were bussed to hear a string quartet
in some asbestos village hall. For once
he didn't knee at kids in front or look round
for the snacks and drinks. He fancied a go
at the violin, varnish glinting under
his jaw, dust raining off horsehair, gouging
wiry nasals out of that bottom string.

'That bloody thing sets my teeth on edge!'
yells his mum at the teacher who's helped him home
with an overloaded bike after hearing his weekly
variation on 'Some twat's taken my music.'

Whenever visitors come to hear a group of them,
his pegs are out or his bow's hanging loose,
and no one bothers asking who's to blame.

ENJOY YOUR FLIGHT

Not my children, but check-in's given me
their bright eyes full of take-off.

They squash their heads into the window,
scrabble through Jet Cadet handouts,
show me overhead signs, buttons
that tilt you, fetch a hostess,
switch channels, make things louder.

Bawled at from behind for flicking
ashtrays and told to leave me be,
they stab at dot-to-dot dinosaurs,
spot some *Missing Words*, then compete
to tap my arm with whispered information.

My wife signals a swop across the gangway.
No thanks. She's got grumblers. The sort
who consult their watches with a sweep
and unwrap complaints like snacks.

ANIMA

'...the insinuations of the anima, the mouthpiece of the unconscious,
can utterly destroy a man...' (C.G. Jung: *Memories, Dreams, Reflections*.)

Once I had to please a presence that moaned
through draughty doors, gave me goosepimples
where the path dipped into Fir Wood,
multiplied my steps under the arch
that guarded Walled Garden.

It was the ghost of Granny Witchwood
who roughed it with oil lamps and goats
at The Kilns. She'd flap back her hood
and wither me with a wicked sneer
from illustrated Grimm.

You could pass off fifty centimes for sixpence,
filch eggs from the henhouse, touch
yourself up. But dare leave the bed rucked,
take a short cut, more pudding, or miss
Mass, and she'd be waiting.

Cooler now and ageless, she stares
through windscreens, nudges me at the mirror,
slips *sotto voice* into the backwaters
of a second thought, and on calm days
rustles in the undergrowth.

PROXIMITIES

for Anne Beresford*

You stood noticing
how trees spoke to themselves
of love;
husks cracked
with another spring,
lovingly.

You spoke someone's name,
hearing it in the air,
half-hoping for an answer.

Or was it
leaves and seeds
falling?

*

I hear a stirring
high among sycamores;
not a breeze, not autumn rattling;

a kind of invitation.
Your voice, perhaps,

echoing round this wide
small world.

* (On reading her poem *Talking to an Absent Friend in the Garden)*

36

FINE AMOUR

'...never dorste he tellen hire his grevaunce...' (The Franklin's Tale)

How to tell her my life's in her hands,
that slip of a woman who broods along cliff tops,
keeps aloof in the dance like a falcon shy of its hood.

Textbook Squire, in love with my Lady,
I look for an answer in eyes settled
on distance. Blurt it out and she'll laugh
without creasing her face, ready with a quest:
the sort Ladies conjure up from nightmares
where plumed shadows charge down the rules.
'Yours if you find the answer, the anodyne.'

Words! We cram ourselves to death with words.
Half starved I malinger in and out of bed
for two prescribed years, nursing a wounded Heart.

WEIGHTS & MEASURES

You wait for two cooking apples,
fumble to oblige with change and watch a couple
        loading a long, blue estate
outside the entrance to the Four Star.

Her endowments are slipped inside
a flowery shirt, *violetly* caressed by leggings.
        Her partner's pony tail tugs
at the roots of his thinning crown.

She's leant towards his goodbye kiss.
The hand that traversed her hips is waving at a tailgate.
        You ache to know if the one
left standing always loves the most.

PASSING THE BUCK

Don't examine those hands or turn them over
as if you're looking for an answer.
Membrane and skin are made to fit
and peel, and there are softer targets.

Their dog, for instance. Men that tinker
all day. Children beserk and untidy,
doors slammed out of habit, the elected
face oozing blarney for your benefit.

Okay, so the world's on offer in packets,
and nextdoor's gadgets are the life and soul
of Sundays. You're a pro now, an armchair
grumbler. What more is there to ask?

TARGETING TOYOTAS

Picking up litter and wondering if
she'll even manage *hello*, I'm buttonholed
and told to lock my Corolla away.

Friday teatime their Landcruiser went.
It had deadlocks, alarm, immobiliser,
everything they could think of. Abroad
by now, the Police reckon. *Not fair, is it,*
going off with other peoples' things?

Agreed. I'm all for brand name solidarity.
But holding on to till our knuckles go white
won't stop the have-nots nicking stuff from
under our noses. It's bereavement with sops
like their Insurance coming up trumps
with a *T Reg*, and so far only two hub caps gone...

ANGOISSSE DE SOCIÉTÉ

They'd like you to go for drinks. Spectres
uncork smiles, dart out unanswerables
slick and powdery as silver fish. My nightmare
attic's inquisitors prickling up the spine
till I leap flights down and wake to a cold
sweat clutching the key no-one surrenders.

I'll stumble through tunnels pinpricked
by light, face a climb with no prospect,
but not half glasses wrinkling hands,
the mutual taste of undigested failures.

Years yawn behind their shoulders
however young or jocular, teetering on
over mine with anguish over what's to come,
and me too scrambled up in it to run.

TURN OF THE TIDE

Exhausted with measuring how or why,
you're drifting out into the current,
and it's beginning to seem the only way.

Whose hair is it letting your fingers
run through? Whose nape does it assume
your palms will surprise with a kind of healing?

Admit that *someone's* steadily drifting
into *somebody* you have long been longing
to tell that this is what you'd like to do.

Though perhaps for once you'll trust to
a lighter touch, leaving words dogged
by scruples to echo in their own compartments.

BETTER UNSAID

Recalling the Upper Belvedere
I recap from Michelin and smile
at its nudge about the works
of Gustav Klimt: '*Note also The Kiss.*'
For you'd prepared me even before
we left the hotel, dashing up
four floors and back for a postcard
to show me how tenderly the man's hands rested.

Yet when we stood before the original,
thawing out from the Price of Savoy's walks,
my eye ran down each pattern of a coverlet
that draped her, till I saw feet pointed
limply at her lover as if to match
her look of comfort and assent.
'Yes. We neglect our feet,' you said
in a voice that told me this was
your moment, and made me want to say
I could ease away the chill from yours.

But his fingers touched without taking,
and the restraint of his bearded lips
warned me not to smother you with fantasies,
so I turned aside with something about
reflexology and Chinese concubines.

SIDELINED

I push through swing doors to Marks and Spenser's,
hold one back for an unsteady, wizened woman who smiles,
followed by a blonde whose mind's on a pushchair.

In *Lingerie* women looking practical bring back
the crackle of static as I'm asked to help a shadow
out of what still clings to her, and into bed.

Then headless on a dummy, a black dress patterned
with silver leaves, finely sprinkled, so like the one
you wore to *The Magic Flute* all those weeks ago.

I miss your hair spiralling darkly to its shoulders,
shoes with matching buckles taken off to stretch your feet,
surprisingly small as I held them through tights.

It's a loose dress, not designed to stun, let alone kill,
innocent as a flag never hoisted in a cause. But now,
forgetting what I came in here to look for, I brush

its crisp folds with a backward sweep, touch the hem
casually as I did when complimenting you that night
in the pub as we unwound from a dose of culture:

and I mean it still, though you're a hundred miles
away, getting on with your life, while I rehearse
a set piece you probably wouldn't recognise.

IMPOSING HARMONIES

The adagios of these Handel vinyls remind me how
pleased you were to find a period performance
for my birthday, though even now the prestos
taunt me with your dig about a single-parent
trainee splashing out on a boxed set of three.

Like their giver these concerti insist
on being heard, on careful handling before
and after. Their nack of cooling fractious
phrases with measured tempi brings back the way
you showed my impatience up for what it was.

*

But there's other music: the airy skirl
of rails at the approach of trains that hurried
you north after a long day's work, having to
park your son and fight the Friday rush.
You'd alight taller than ever, unaware
of heads turned, relieved to find me there.

Now my pulse races for someone coming south,
you'd say I've merely rearranged my spots.
Waiting where I half meant to end things
by refusing your goodbye kiss, I still
throttle myself with dreams of closeness
no self-respecting lover's going to match.

MORE *THIS* THAN *THAT?*

...dialogue is the only respectable way of contradicting yourself...

(Tom Stoppard)

Trying to please is a recipe for
resentment stirred and refined
by time. Personal hygiene, your own
teeth, and an eye for what to wear,
carry no clout. Least of all with those
who should be safe investments.

Who's looking at that torso
you've kept so flat, at legs
an elderly German woman behind you
on a climb to Bismarck's monument,
called *Strengbeine*? Not so much strong
as lean and toned for action.

There are no eyes to caress
the hair that should by now
be going down the plughole fast.
And whose fingers will tug at it
for dear life as wave after wave
sweeps insatiably on?

You'd unleash a pack of quibbles
if you didn't shrink from having to
stand by them, hold fast
to your rock while others sail past
at their own pace, dock or launch off
to destinies that must be better.

STAGING POST

I should lean absent-mindedly on all
this sky and sea but seeing far and wide
shows that what we long for yet fear most
is permanence. Not that I can say so,
and sensing, perhaps, that I'm off my guard
up here, you start on alterations.

Our three-piece is an inherited fire hazard;
but first let's demolish what divides where
we used to sit and eat, from lolling and TV,
merge the greasy galley kitchen via pillars
with the uninspiringly square 'utility',
upgrade our cubic capacity.

I wonder if this is how you put time
on hold, investing in a fresh start. More likely
your broad feet are in touch with the ways
and means of *terra firma*, and I'm one of
the unwary who deserve to be overtaken
for letting things be, rot if they will.

This air's good for talk and outlines.
I sway to your virtuoso clarity: theme-
option-repeat-surprise-reprise, rondo
that never exhausts itself. But somehow
details swim off into what my wilting
faith calls *oceans of probability*.

PLAYING WITH FLOWERS

Just when everything's tidy and needs
no coaxing you come up with packets of seeds
I might like to try; and I can't resist.
Their touched-up promise of colour, that crisp,
fizzy rattle reminds me of fireworks
I'd fondle for days before the event
as if they had a life of their own.

But this year's sunflowers will be
the limit, surely. Lashing them bit by bit
to eight foot canes won't hold them tight
in the August gales, and the best heads
hanging swollen beyond help, snap off
without opening. If we'd provide
the sun they'd live up to their name.

But others rally, all calyx and no petal,
looking away over the wall they've topped,
afterthoughts sown where they'd caught
a backblast and had to stretch for light.

WORTH ITS WEIGHT

I trudge through resisting shingle
to shed the fear that fear of
anything *beyond* insists
there's nothing more than
what we track and weigh,
my head so full of stones
I stumble over lovers
who've forgotten the tide.

Then I start to pick up hearts
(though none are what they seem)
until I chance on one that sparkles
even after drying, and promises
to please you with more than shape,
as if belonging gives another
life to what the sea has worn.

Brought home it's smiled at,
shelved, even dusted, but too
innocently sure of its place
to be just another token
slipped into a drawer, then out
with anything that fades, goes dog-eared,
or was once worn for love.

NO UNDERTOW

Most of all I'd miss your silences.
They let us breathe across prairies and chasms
without a hint of separation

No brooding retreat into some sea
of your own. More like the sea itself
that expects nothing, does not ask
to be encountered, notice the frailties
that trust their luck to it or gauge
the pause between each unintended surge.

Having somewhere to flow to you're not
moved to divert me from the way I am:
maker of spurious paths straddling
supposed horizons only to fall
back on your immeasurable swell.

3

HELIOTROPIC

ALEGRO CON MUCHO JUGO

For Max Hamilton

Hala-para-valerse-de-melon-y-cocoloco!
It might be a call to prayer pitched
above yells and surf when sun's
at its peak and there's drought
on the wind: his trays of uncut
fruit the one oasis in this desert.

Five foot mahogany, he draws
disciples into a semi-circle
from sea games and parasols,
refining his tremulo between
orders like a bird grown taller
in song. He hammers coconuts

three times, shakes down the milk,
and offers a perfect brimming half.
Quick as a signature the skewer-thin
blade has diced the rest on his thigh,
and gutted a quarter of flesh-pink Melon.
And they think they've followed every twist.

Anana-tuttifruti-vitimina-potencia!
He's doubling back for pineapples
on feet that never touch the sand
to a stack more than twice his size,
spirited there along the rocks,
inviolable as a bag of tricks.

Note: The title translates from the Spanish as '*An Allegro with plenty of Juice*'. The
snatches of song can be ruined as follows: '*Come and take advantage of my melon and
coconut*'... & ... '*Pineapple, pure fruit, rich in vitamins.*'

ESPRESSO

This strong coffee tastes of you.
Sharing it we feel our elbows
meet across the beach bar.
Dark tongues slip suggestions
over the shallows and into a deeper blue.

A lone drinker squints at the last of his beer
and flicks for a waitress, trying not to size up others
smiling round their tables.
A family enterprise in polka-dot blue.

I touch the sun wrinkles
round your eyes.
Your cigarette's reflective.
Easily confessional, these
minutes lift us bodily into widening blue.

OUT OF TUNE

Tracks of blackbird song are frequencies
that won't erase, echoing from sides
of a scrub-littered rift in rock:
dry watercourse no developer would touch,
but handy amplifier for a bird singing
from expatriate British gardens.

I'm pierced again for the first time
by something grown familiar. More like taste
than sound it splits apart cadences
of traffic, arguments from balconies,
cleaners sweeping broken glass, and if I hold
my breath everything will shut up and listen.

SHADY PATHS

It's dusk and I'm under exotic trees
where a bird's improvising so fiercely
it breaks new particles of sound. Worth
a stop after trudging through whitewashed suburbs
with their bougainvillaea, banana bushes,
and runabouts stuffed with aquabatic gear.

Yet anyone coming round the corner
might wonder why I seem to be intent
on vacancies between branches. A nutter
or loitering with intent? Lucky then
for the woman with a souvenir bag of shopping,
that this dense clump divides the path.

She switches with practised indifference
to the longer loop as I surface to
raucous laughter, a whiff of stirfry,
three designer youths busy over bar prices,
and find I'm walking fast to a One Way
where endless pairs of lights take aim.

BONANZA PACKAGES

MONEY

Flattened against against stuffed-toy stalls,
a little girl's still clutching the note
she can't think how to spend.

A used face cools its temples
on the tinted glass of a sporty Ford,
eyes blank as soiled coins looking through
patches of sweat on outsize T-shirts, droves
of shorts-plus twosomes, families
lugging each other every way at once
round menus and bric-à-brac.

Those ready for a spurt of purpose, tighten
their marsupial purses and devour
arterial tarmac into a brochure sunset.

EUCHARISTIC

Under a rakish quarter moon
families sit and eat outside
time. Waiters are a caste that mutters
to itself, favouring each table through teeth
perfect as stars.

Time to drink to happiness and take
acquaintance down a peg or two. They're trailing worlds
beyond this glow.

Dishes and wines are rites unvaried
since time began. Queries only
show how easily truth is missed.
Every dish is succulent, every sauce subtler
than its name.

Partners and offspring were never so pliant,
or waited on so warmly with liqueurs and blessings
for the road.

VOYEURS

Face down her lines grace evergreen
lilo with a tanned sheen.
Her jazzy double tickles
the pool's meticulous tiles.
Her strokes shimmer with ripples that lap
at her as we do, three floors up.

AERIAL

Jets swoop at sandy inlets of sunny
families, their blue, blue ocean green
from those cockpits.

Consider somewhere further east:
the flip of a wing and five second burst
leaves them swimming in blood.

Here it's a Sunday pastime
to rocket marinas dotted with sunshades
and white flotillas.

HOTEL PARADISO

Dawn Cast-Off

He paces the balcony like a ship's captain,
shiny cap and zoom lenses commanding the view.
  With a yell that sounds like *Sweepshee*
he's making waves and pointing out to sea.
  No-one follows his aim. Whether he's discovered
new folds and fissures on the next island,
  or spotted dolphins looping through the sound,
a summons from the wheelhouse ends his voyage.
  His wife's mapping out another day that began
with hatches open and rations ready for 7 a.m..

Breakfast with Maria

A tiny owl creaks like a stiff door hinge
and two gulls wheel so high they are black,
screech twice at each other and move south.

One large man sits under a Pepsi sunshade
baring the torso of a singed boar over shorts
tight as chastity. He's ready to start on
how he and his mates were finally chucked out
at 2 a.m., how Lanzarote's better for twelve
hour sprees: but he booked this place the day
the brochure came out, just to give it a go.

Maria's genuflecting to prise chips
from the outside freezer and gets
his husky *What-sort-of-time's-this-
to-start-my-breakfast?* She flashes her
Buenos Días, hoists a screen, unwinds
the awning and wipes the tops before
he's thought of what to order

MERIDIAN

Palm fronds like cockerel tails rattle
to a passing thermal. *Pock-pack-pock-hock*
goes the tennis on exclusive surfaces.
Zikka-zakka-zum-zi's the bar's noon number
synthesised on Mildly Orgasmic.

Pinning a bunch of drinkers to their sunbeds
with another yarn, the poolside Number One
adjusts his azure satin trunks and turns
a broad, hairy back to the sun.

Immaculate blue is dutifully furrowed. Wives collect
a drop or two, elegantly testing the temperature.

Far out in the bay a speed boat
churns out Sixty Nines on the sea's
slate, turning back to fill up.

OFF COURSE

A neatly-bearded old man sits up from sunning himself,
smiles and reaches for a palm-size jotter.
Who's to know if it's for notes on shopping,
an agenda, or the hotel's pros and cons?
Fixed on a glossy creeper's pendulous pinks
he writes in spurts with crossings out.

Nothing could ruffle him till flesh explodes
its weight in water, bringing him back to
a baby's whimper, children making decisions
round the *Ice Cream*, a tabby lapping
chlorinated puddles and overhead a hawk's
limpid wing and tail tips turning to bronze,
as his lounger sails him into evening.

HELIOTROPIC

They've flown four hours south into
light, but taking to the skies seemed
less of a risk than being together.

Over makeshift breakfast, stunned
by the clarity of things, they look
at one another's lives for what they are,

exchanging doubts like real voyagers
who see that going it alone through
a mess of hazards can make or break.

Now this woman who scarcely moved
in her own darkness is one he dares
tongue through a T-Shirt, and she
surprises him with *yes*, shedding
her scales to coil him back.

MAKING UP

Nights-out remind him of party balloons
still bobbing out of reach. He's seen men
smartened up, tagging along, determined that lights
and events mean fun; women trim as winged
yachts kept on course by their own currents.

More or less the way it's been with him and her
as they climb back several palpitating flights
and he hears *Let's go to bed*, or was it
I'm going to bed? No fumbling for lights,
no comment till she says he took no persuading.

MADE IN HEAVEN

My travellers' cheques are sellotaped
behind that pastel of a mountain village
I hadn't looked at. Now its flecks of red
creeper sprout from rock too violently,

making me wonder if the heavy traffic
jars you, lying on the apartment's plastic
settee, struck by sciatica just as the Easter
sun topped the Los Gigantes cliffs,

though you smile bravely at warmth
longed for two thousand miles ago,
till the next spasm flares. Then lines
I think I've never seen tighten your face.

Slumped beside you I run out of things
to say; but my hands fidget for answers
with a dry, helpless sound. Canaries sing past:
a sweetness we could share this far

from the childrens' worries, and days
when gadgets break, leak, or cost money.
But pain sparkles like a force field
and you're spinning away behind it.

A DARKER LINING

Awake in the small hours what if we could
probe each other's thoughts, the reverse
shadowy side of what we keep saying to sound
as if we believe it?

Lying there I walk out, take any train
to where it ends up, unpack my longings,
look back at ties like lines on a map,
take days as they come.

It's the spider me watching the insect
me daring to suppose that I can do
anything I like as easily as that,
whenever I choose.

But trying to unravel you, I tangle with half-
truths that cut more cruelly than not knowing.

4

OUTSTRIPPING GRAVITY

OCTOBER DIRGE

...or son venuto
là dove molto pianto mi percute. (Dante: Inf.V,26)

For a child of seven what dead stalk the night?
Halloween's her gutted pumpkin christened
Peter and powered by a stub of candle to hang
on the washing line. She's tiptoe on a chair
pressing the window pane to enjoy the fear
of a grin that flickers to and fro in the night.

Those triangle eyes are trinities of hell
tinting the mist geese howl through, heading
east from lake to lake to feed all night.
And two who've lost their bearings
wail from far behind, weighing me down
with wings that cannot beat the night.

Father's ghost smokes away the night,
going over and over why *she* had to die.
Slumped over an armchair meal he needs
another change of blood. But mother's dying
three floors up, terrified of what's beyond
estuary lights that dance away the night.

'LIGHT OF COMMON DAY'*

You stopped skipping into the wind
to tell me you'd never again see your lake
    with its seven swans in a bowl
of hills. 'Dreams can return', I said,
    my mind on last-minute shopping,
half-catching what you'd said about the silence.

But holding your hand to cross a main road
    I longed for you to make it back.
Gaps between cars yawned and closed. Jumping
    over white lines you nearly tripped.
Even sunlight flitting across a wall warned me
    not to take your words for granted.

Later the wind dropped. I looked in on you
    sleeping through heavy traffic,
and the moon looked in as it began to sink
    in vaporous cloud. Perhaps that made me
tamper with your swans and turn them into souls
    released from having to return.

But when I asked as casually as I could
    if you'd been to your valley again,
you were matter-of-fact. The lake was a river
    carrying you away to be drowned
till swans became ducks and tugged you
    towards a kind of roundabout.

* The title derives from Wordsworth's *Intimations of Immortality* (Stanza 5)

MORNING AFTER

The Sunday ringers are practising muffled repeats
as I scatter tealeaves round a dried-up rose.
In the shop a regular sheds her supplements
slamming the tactics of the press.

The lovers are on Page Three yachting against a sea
of troubles. She's thickening, he's bald and pallid,
but they play the old game, all set for Paris.

The kitchen radio's playing a piano monody.
Special programming, I'm told. An accident
too late for the *Sundays*.

Blame the lens for not matching the hype,
and they come in close enjoying what's left,
but rush beyond our reach towards a heap
of steel and plastic.

DREAM PARTINGS

I end a phone call meant for news
with longings you choose
to ignore, having no use
for frailties or shadows.

Cloud streams along the mountain
but you walk drenched in sun.
Your smile parting the rain
tells me there's nowhere to run.

So we drift on down the valley,
you skimming heather and scree
while I give way to doubts
and trip over scrub and roots.

Then grass glistens, a fox flares
in the green and coolly disappears;
I shout as if you could hear,
fields away from my fear.

FUGITIVE

Her smile was a fugue
I could not unravel.
Fathoms down
an intention wept,

her cheek cold
as a succuba
when I laid mine to it
and thought a hot current
must race below the ice:

but where she should be moist
the watercourse ran dry

*

Then she turned away
and with her went the key.

Waking was a chord
unresolved, suspending me
like a bird
with wings half-spread.

EASING THE CAST

He's plaster from head to pelvis,
arms limp below his solid biceps.

O the flexing of her shoulders and hips
as she screens him off for the once-over,
whisking back the sheet to discover
the urge he cannot hold or fold away.

Her smile goes practical
and misty; the curtains swell
like lungs, their rings go dancing through her hair,
till stars burst from his equator,
spattering the air,
draining the world
of its weight.

'Nice one', she says. 'Lucky
we didn't have to set that.'

GREEN PAPER

Deck chair, sun and air seem best
for skimming pages packed with clauses,
notwithstandings, options,
whole lives set out like equations
that slither round tax factors.

I look up and see two pansies
shake with laughter in the breeze,
bearded faces weighing me up
through a grill of laser-printed
type that's inked my cornea.

They change their looks in hours.
Words take centuries to shrink
or grow new shoots, unless we pick,
mix and dry them into husks.

OPUS WHAT?

Radio's blurred hours at the screen,
tapping in and out one lot of words
after another, chasing some voice
that won't be heard, cobbling chunks
to look like stanzas, all for shadows
already breathing down my neck
with how they're lost or what to cut.

Finish Edit. Power Off. Catch
the first, slow bars of some quartet.
Draw breath with the violins before
they go *vivace*. Prance about sketching
phrases in the air, absurdly alive.

AFTER THE WORKSHOP

for John Forth

Childhoods in verse make it feel unsafe
to be a passenger, bends swallowing double-white,
our wheels frail as stitched-on buttons.

Then we're neon-lit past perimeters
of transit depots chained to a town
with little going on after steel.

'*A hard place*,' you say, slamming it with every
gear change, swinging your tirade round
islands till it swells to anatomies of dark

so palpable down narrow lanes our main beam
can't be cutting us back to places somehow
set apart because we call them *home*.

TASKS

For Herbert Lomas

No sooner had I dreamed your good
wishes in *Selected Poems* than
quibblers feathered into reeds,
and swept me from my path across
a marsh to wake dry-mouthed
thinking about glossy-covered verse
we'd stacked in graded heaps:

like sorting stones from shingle banks
the sea flings up. No stickler for tasks,
it may or may not break the backs
of tankers crawling from pane to pane
as we sit down to our lives.

Committees in love with sitting on verse
and eating air should meet
by the sea like allnight anglers, feel
aeons pluck, earth's gills make
and unmake in a breath, waves pounding
decisions on stone.

Make your seventies apart:
go up a floor and leave them all guessing.
The stones you dream about are words,
shining at the tide's edge. Once dry
they're no more than stone.

FESTAL VICTIM

She's smiling, pleased to be up there,
knowing how a long-awaited book of verse
becomes a legend in advance:
but it's a smile full of teeth,
and there's grievance at the corners,
a thrust of vendetta in that chin.
Miss this and a hint of vixen
sniffing for advantage
and the gazelle eyes could take you in.
Even as she sifts out recent work
and says her writing is domestic,
a way of giving shape to twists and turns,
the adrenalin's pumping what's unsaid.

So it's a relief when bobbed hair
perfectly platinum shakes into place,
her face tops the lectern,
cheek muscles slacken
and the poetry has its say.

MOZART'S MOVEMENTS

Regina Strinasacchi. With a name
like that, and a violin under
her Mantuan chin, how could her tour
fall flat? Unlikely in Vienna,
whose spies were booking maturer
talent than prodigies raised
to play on a winched-up dais.

Hearing her prepare to enthral
the pundits and court, *his* clientèle,
he moved in with an offer
she couldn't refuse: a sonata
matching her finesse, *from one
who'd be honoured to grace her debut
by following from the fortepiano.*

She got her part the morning before.
On the night he was a stream
that knew its course, letting her
dance above and beyond. Whatever
the Emperor's glasses lighted on,
the piano score he asked to see
was a sheaf of empty staves.

THRESHOLD

A half-smile at the door, you're shorter than ever,
more pinched, as if the years and all the others
have taken you for granted. You know why I'm here,
so perhaps the misted-over half's a pause
to weigh me up or hold back in case I turn away.

Your door's ghost-grey and flaking. Catching the eye
of its stained-glass diamond, I feel I'm here for you.
But your fingers, terribly long for one so small,
will knead my superfluous aches before you probe
your own disquiet to touch me where it hurts.

HYPNOSIS

I strode downhill
        making for the wood
        as you said I should.
Trees stood still

to open a track.
        A cuckoo caressed
        the distance; lost
foothills broke

the shade, lifting me
        where faces stare,
        voices sift the air
and you're leaving me

to find another way,
        shouldering old
        shadows into the gold
of a clearer day.

ELEMENTALS

'...healing would imply the deenergising of elementals working within the subconscious...' (from Spiros Sathi's words in K.C. Markides' *Fire in the Heart*)

Darken a room, light
  a white candle between
    salt and water, and sit
      before that flame until
        no face, no passing
          phrase or picture
            pierces its blade.

      Blow it out to burn
     on, and through it
    pass every grudge,
   fear or urge, casting
  their dross in salt,
 cleanser from earth
they've invaded.

Scatter it outside,
  broadly, for it burns.
    Drink in three draughts
      water charged with cure:
        the power of One,
          Wisdom's breath,
            the Healer's touch.

COLOUR THERAPIST

'My friend died of the cancer she'd never admit.
There's this divorce; and the man I love walks out...
But all paths lead to God.
Whatever you feel, imagine you're kissing
other people's feet. We must acknowledge
our bodies, care for them.
Cleanse your anguish with the violet flame
of the Comte de St Germain reborn many times,
the blue of Archangel Michael.'

*

Set off by a black dress
your necklaces and bracelets
are everywhere at once
like flames among the hotel's
after-breakfast fuss.

Earthed by a scaffold of bones,
visions are eating you.
I watch your eyelids flutter,
a mouth making love to
words illuminating presences.

Your Ex appears, impervious
behind his chunky olive shirt,
on time for the encounter
that's slipped your mind.

A MATTER OF TURNOVER

'...Simon the pharisee asked Jesus to a meal with him...' (Luke, 7.36)

She'd heard about his stunt outside the gates,
snatching some boy from a hearse, the widowed mother
dumb with disbelief. Good for trade, swelling
the streets with those who milked the crowd
and could be made to pay for her in silver.

But the way he stooped among the riff raff
jammed her signals. Her usual clients went on
pretending she wasn't there. But she wasn't.
Something like butterflies but more barbed
took over, turning her inside out.

*

After he'd spoken she was swept along
to the smart quarter, past rows of sandals
politely abandoned outside dinners, part show,
part feast, where men reclined like gentiles,
while the dregs and hangers-on scavenged
for scraps of meat and talk.

He lay away from from her, attentive to
to the pharisee who gave him Rabbi treatment.
She could gauge a man from any angle, weigh up
the risks and pluses, tell how he rated himself.
So what was it that eluded her sums, her hard-
earned business principles?

*

But his host grew tired of a seer who looked
servants in the eye, gave you practical replies,
then didn't seem to know what kind of woman
was attending to his feet with fake tears
and hair, rubbing in enough of that ill-gotten
ointment to prepare a dozen wedding guests.

But why turn round when he could see it all
and more on the *official* face? Not much
to distinguish the whore and the high-ranker
when it came to counting the cost, and yet
in the silence of her tears, wet enough
on his feet, her face was not for sale.

ONE OF THE FOLD

'The Faith' ferments behind doors
you think you've shut. Feel it
burn when your snigger can't deflect
the blow a real agnostic lands you
in fair and square vernacular.

Its Days and taboos cling
like the priest who still calls,
asks you to pray with him, or leaves
a card of the Holy Family in haloes
and long robes that somehow stain
your resolve to wash the car.

Like a bottle you've not given up,
it hides, only to leap out with that
familiar oldbrew, kicking you up a gear
past every hang-up to where it all connects
and flowers and candles are just so.

ABSOLUTION

Car round the clock and overdue for service,
I sit among gleaming saloons and hatches,
five figure offers ending in three nines.
Beasts that look as if at the slightest touch,
they'd stretch to please you with their outlines,
prelapsarian, but for their bums and grins:
too human, like the rite of passage they wait for.
*Do you take this car to be your lawful
vehicle till part-exchange?*
                              Not me! I fall
back on *Trouble Shooting* patter, the way
the *Key of Heaven*'s checklists helped
me dress up sins for visits to the grille;
put up with piped Pop, ding-dong demands
for someone in *Parts* or *Sales*, dream
of feeling clean in body and soul,
the worksheet flush with ticks.

Note: *The Key of Heaven* was a Roman Catholic manual of prayer that included a pre-confessional Examination of Conscience, listing possible sins under various headings.

NO ONE*

Bearing witness to truth's absence
he promises no profit, cannot play
the role of crying in the wilderness.
For what's made straight by denying
equations solved at a button's touch?
What's made manifest by demanding proofs
of the Machine's miraculous performance?

Like the moon phasing itself out
over Llŷn he turns away from borrowed
certainties. His voice rings with open
spaces whose peaks and troughs diminish
history. His seas ruminate without
conclusion, and whatever broods between
light and Light answers to no name.

* This was particularly inspired by a close reading of R.S. Thomas' *Laboratories of the Spirit (1975)*

80

MAKING FOR ABERCUAWG*

In mem: J.R.R.T.

'Grandfather's outside,' I'm told. It's meant
to be a dream but I make him wear what I never
dared call his *God-of-Ages* frown that goes with
waving a stick and shouting on my behalf:
"Leave the lad be: he's work to do!"

A room too low for his liking is too dim
for me to grasp who or what is in my way.
Far off a telephone chirrups accusingly,
and banging closer in quick succession
doors open and shut as if to make a point.

Then we're crossing water-meadows where weeds
and willows won't keep their shapes and he's
after a butterfly, maroon with gilded veins
and fringes. With a wily grin he names it
in Welsh, catching us both without a net.

I remember the phrase like a tune, trusting him
to say it stands for *Hair of Llewelyn's Daughter*.
'Whoever she was, her soul is schooled at any flower.
Surely you can hear her whisper round those reeds
more softly than the cuckoos of Abercuawg?'

* *Abercuawg* ('Aberkeeaoog') is a utopian place alluded to in a 9th century Welsh
metric cycle: '*Yn Abercuawg yt ganant gogeu...*'

OUTSTRIPPING GRAVITY

For Robert Turner: 1946-1998

The night of the day I now know you'd died
thousands of miles north of here, I couldn't
face the mad frown of the full tropical moon.
Any moment it would rise from its false-
dawn glow on the rim of cliffs that billow
behind avenues twinkling tier after tier
to exclusive crests.

Had I faced it as I try to in memory of you,
would I have felt anger and confusion
in your spirit, its need to return to the earth
willingly left in perfect turbulence
twenty years to the day after you'd first
shouldered the odds against touching down
from serious bird games?

Not for you that transit jail of ghosts
suspended in their manias and longings,
who once or twice a year stampede toward
us when the tug of waters breaks their bounds.
Only your body dropped, intact but or a bruise
on the nose you said was a nuisance
at icy altitudes.

Hard to believe the morning after the news,
the moon swimming on its back as I paddle
through black sand and the sea's indifference,
till one gull stands its ground then scales sheer
rock without straps, cramp, crackling radio
or freak eddy to crumple the kite that makes it
lighter than air,

circling like you to cherish our screwed-up
searches and the lives your vision changed,
before soaring into the unexplored on thermals
no bird dreamed of but you had practised:
as if for the long cruise from which you may
come burning back to teach us in other ways
that heights depend on scale and there's more
to flight than flying.